Savior in the Manger

WRITTEN BY **SYLVIA NANTONGO**

EDITED BY **DR. JOHN MILLER**

AuthorHouse™
1663 Liberty Drive
Bloomington, IN 47403
www.authorhouse.com
Phone: 1 (800) 839-8640

Published by AuthorHouse 10/24/2018

ISBN: 978-1-5462-6006-6 (hc)
ISBN: 978-1-5462-6004-2 (e)

Library of Congress Control Number: 2018911192

Print information available on the last page.

Any people depicted in stock imagery provided by Getty Images are models, and such images are being used for illustrative purposes only. Certain stock imagery © Getty Images.

This book is printed on acid-free paper.

authorHOUSE®

Savior in the Manger

LOVE & LEARN

··

LITTLE STAR KIDS'
Inspirational Books

··

A young man called Yusuf from Judea, Israel got

engaged to a young, and virgin girl Maria.

Maria was beautiful, and innocent, and she had never

been in any relationship with a man.

Yusuf was good, and an honest man too.

Just before they got married, Maria became pregnant in a miraculous way.

She had a special child in her womb with the help of the power of God.

Yusuf became confused, and wanted to abandon

Maria because of her mysterious pregnancy.

The angel appeared to Yusuf in a dream, and told him not

to be afraid of taking Maria as his wife because the baby

she had in her womb was of the power of God.

The baby was the promised Messiah foretold by the prophets in the Bible.

He is the Savior in the manger.

The angel said to Yusuf that the child would be called Emmanuel

meaning, "God is with us"-, and He would save the whole world.

Emmanuel would be King of the universe.

Yusuf woke up from sleep, and he went, and married Maria.

Maria was happy to be pregnant with the miracle baby in her womb.

He is the Savior in the manger.

Maria had a song because she was blessed to have this baby, and she was highly favored among women, and the child she was going to bear was blessed too.

Maria's song

"My soul glorifies the Lord

And my spirit rejoices in God my Savior

For He has been mindful of the humble state of His servant

From now on all generations will call me blessed,

For the Mighty One has done great things for me

Holy is His name

His mercy extends to those who fear Him

from generation to generation

He has performed mighty deeds with His arm

He has scattered those who are proud in their inmost thoughts

He has brought down rulers from their thrones

But has lifted up the humble

He has filled the hungry with good things

But has sent the rich away empty.

He has helped his servant Israel

Remembering to be merciful

to Abraham, and his descendants forever

Just as he promised our ancestors."

One day, Yusuf, and Maria went for a national registration in Bethlehem

because everyone from that city was required to register.

While in Bethlehem, Maria started having labor pains because

she was ready to give birth to the miracle baby Emmanuel.

Maria gave birth to her firstborn Emmanuel, and

wrapped Him in swaddling clothes.

She laid Him in the manger because there was no room for them in the hotel.

He is the Savior in the manger.

There was a group of country shepherds who took care

of sheep, and watched over them during night.

The angel appeared to them with lightening, and they were greatly afraid!

The angel told them not to be afraid because he had brought for

them good news, and joy which would be for all people.

He told them that a special child had been born on that

day, and He would be the Savior of the world.

He is the Savior in the manger.

Suddenly, there was an army of heavenly angels singing

"Glory to God in the highest

Peace, and good will towards people."

When the angels went back to heaven, the shepherds said to themselves.

"Let us go to Bethlehem, and see the new born

baby that the angel has told us about."

The shepherds were led by the star from the east to Bethlehem

where baby Emmanuel was lying in the manger with His parents.

The star came, and stood where baby Emmanuel was.

The wise men rejoiced with great joy, and fell on their

faces, and worshipped baby Emmanuel!

They opened their treasures, and presented Gold,

Frankincense, and myrrh to Him as gifts.

Then the wise men went their way singing, rejoicing, and spread the

good news about the birth of the miraculous baby Emmanuel.

He is the Savior in the manger.

There was a king in that city called Herod who hated

baby Emmanuel because he was a jealous king.

King Herod had asked the wise men to go find out where the new born

baby was, and go back, and tell him because He wanted to kill Him.

But the wise men never went back to king Herod

to tell him where baby Emmanuel was.

They instead returned to their country in another way as

they had been warned by the angel in the dream.

When king Herod saw that the wise men had deceived him, he was very angry!

He then killed all the male children in Bethlehem, and

in all the districts from two years old, and under because

he thought baby Emmanuel was among them.

He is the Savior in the manger.

The angel appeared to Yusuf again, and told him to take Emmanuel

to Egypt because King Herod wanted to destroy Him.

Then Yusuf, and Maria fled to Egypt, Africa because

king Herod wanted to kill their Son Emmanuel.

But when king Herod died, the angel appeared to Yusuf

again in Egypt, and told him to return to Israel because

king Herod who wanted to kill Emmanuel had died.

They went, and lived in Galilee in the city of Nazareth in Israel.

Emmanuel grew up in body, and in wisdom.

He was loved by God, and people.

He was very compassionate, kind, and loving.

He did many signs, miracles, and wonders.

He healed the sick, the deaf, and the blind.

He raised the dead, and fed the hungry.

He is the Savior in the manger.

But at about **33** years of age, Emmanuel died a terrible death.

He took our pain, and sorrow upon Himself.

He was beaten for our sake, and by His stripes we are healed.

His garment was shared among men, and He

was led as a lamb to be slaughtered.

But He was silent, and He did not open His mouth.

He is the Savior in the manger.

Emmanuel was crucified on the cross between two

robbers. We call that day good Friday.

Yet He had done no violence, and there were no lies in His mouth.

He humbly gave His soul unto death for us, and

He took the sins of many people.

He is the Savior in the manger.

Emmanuel was buried, but on the third day, He came

out of the grave. We call that day Easter.

He appeared to His friends, and followers.

And then He went up to heaven to be with His Father. He is waiting to

come again to judge the whole world. He is the Savior in the manger.

Emmanuel's kingdom brings justice, and peace in the world.

He is the bright morning star, and the morning glory.

He is the rock of ages, and the ancient of days.

He is the lion of the tribe of Judah, and the everlasting God.

He is the Alpha, and Omega, the beginning, and the end.

He is the first, and the last, the one who was, who is, and who will be.

He is the Savior in the manger.

Emmanuel's Kingdom shall not pass away.

He is the King of all the nations.

We will speak about His greatness to all generations.

Every knee will bow before Him, and every tongue will confess that He is Lord.

He will rule forever, and ever.

He is the Savior in the manger.

For unto us a Child is born.

Unto us a Son is given.

And the government will be upon His shoulder.

And His name will be called

wonderful, counselor, mighty God,

everlasting Father, Prince of Peace,

Emmanuel, God is with us.

He is the Savior in the manger!

About the Author

Sylvia Nantongo is from Uganda, East Africa, and she is a graduate of Elim Bible Institute and College Lima, NY. She has an Associate Degree in Science in Biblical, and Theological Studies, and a certificate in Applied Ministry majoring in youth service, and pedagogy. She has a diploma in elementary French language from Alliance Française Kampala, Uganda, and she speaks Luganda, English, French, and Swahili.

Sylvia worked with kids, and youth in Uganda since 2005, and she is now working with Honeoye Falls–Lima Central School District as a Cougar Care staff, and a paraprofessional. She is a youth leader, and a Sunday School teacher at Elim Gospel Church–Lima, and she volunteers as a counselor in different Christian children's camps. She loves spending time with kids, helping them grow mentally, emotionally, and empowering them to realize their full potential. She is also a Barista, and she enjoys cooking, going to the beach, writing, and singing.

Printed in the United States
By Bookmasters